TABLE OF

RE-THINKING THREE ACT STRUCTURE

Hello, and thank you for purchasing our screenwriting book — "Master Sequences". As the title suggests, this book moves on from traditional structure theory to expose how screenplays are actually formed using plot points under the surface of the traditional three acts. By the end of this book you will see three act structure in a whole new light. You may ask what's wrong with the light it's already in? Vague notions of plot abound in the world of screenwriting: "A screenplay is made up of three acts: Act Three, (set-up) Act Two, (development) and Act Three (climax)". "A catalyst has to occur around page twelve". "At the Midpoint the stakes are raised", and so on. All well and good, but we think this approach is a little random. Free-floating, even. Maybe there's something else? Something going on under the broad strokes of three act structure that anchors the plot points and makes it easier to create continuous conflict in the protagonist's journey? Well, there is… Sequences.

Maybe you already use sequences in your writing, but are still unaware of the intricacies involved in how they work? Or perhaps you've heard of sequences, but never used them before? In either case, this book is for you. Over the next seventy or so pages, we will equip you with the knowledge required to revolutionize your understanding of structure via sequences, making conflict easier to understand and, ultimately, easier to write.

JUST WHAT IS A SEQUENCE?

HOW ACTS ARE BROKEN DOWN INTO SEQUENCES, AND SEQUENCES INTO SEGMENTS

Traditional teaching about screenplay structure focuses on classic three act structure that goes something like this: Act One shows a protagonist getting called to a journey, Act Two tracks them going on the journey, and Act Three is the result of that journey — generally coming back home with new lessons learned, and maybe a new relationship too. This structure, however, can be broken down into a much simpler form comprising of seven or eight sequences. (Although in some "epics" such as Lawrence of Arabia, there may be nine or ten.) These sequences underpin the existing three acts like this: two go in Act One, four in Act Two, and one (or two) in Act Three.

Here's how traditional three act structure looks when sequences are added:

ACT ONE: SEQUENCES A AND B

ACT TWO: SEQUENCES C, D, E, AND F

ACT THREE: SEQUENCES G AND H

Each of these sequences can be viewed as a "mini movie" with a specific goal for the protagonist and a resolution that takes him or her further or nearer to achieving the overall goal for the screenplay. Each sequence also has the same three act structure as the overall screenplay, with the climax to each equalling a major turning point in the screenplay.*

In five out of the seven or eight sequences, this major turning point is the same plot point as an act break. We give each sequence a letter, and break it down like this:

SEQUENCE A: CALL TO ACTION

SEQUENCE B: BIG EVENT DECISION

SEQUENCE C: DECISION SUCCESS/FAILURE

SEQUENCE D: MIDPOINT

SEQUENCE E: MIDPOINT SUCCESS/FAILURE

SEQUENCE F: ALL IS LOST/ALL IS JOY

SEQUENCE G: CLIMAX OR ALL IS LOST/ALL IS JOY SUCCESS/ FAILURE

SEQUENCE H: DENOUEMENT OR CLIMAX

This is where some of the confusion between seven and eight sequences arises — when some people prefer to call the scene after the Climax a new "sequence". True, the Climax is a major plot point, but the scene immediately after it is just the Denouement, and after that the credits roll so it's not really a sequence in the true sense of the word.

ANATOMY OF A SEQUENCE

Just as in the overall film, the protagonist's fortunes go from a positive to a negative (or vice-versa) from sequence to sequence as they traverse the screenplay. It's this back and forth motion of each sequence ending alternately on a positive or a negative that gives a screenplay its feel of a "roller-coaster ride". For instance, Sequence E ends on a high point and is followed by a low point of Sequence F at the end of Act Two. This sets up the grand finale of Sequence G: a high point and the climax to the script.

Similarly, the protagonist's fortunes change within the sequence itself, from a positive to a negative (or vice-versa), also helping to create a sense of motion and change. So, if the sequence begins on a high point — Indiana Jones enters the Well of Souls having found the location of the ark, for example — the chances are it'll end on a low point: the Nazis steal the ark and lock him in the Well of Souls with Marion.

HOW SEQUENCES WORK WITHIN MOST FILMS

SEQUENCE A — CD 7

A screenplay often starts (but not always) with an Inciting Incident to get it rolling: either a major change in the protagonist's life, such as just getting out of prison, or arriving in a new town, or an event unknown to them, such as a murder the detective is yet to hear about. Then, characters and world are introduced followed by a crisis around pages ten to fifteen. This is the hero's Call to Action which sets into motion the main conflict for the overall screenplay and ends the sequence.

(In *Romancing the Stone*, Joan hears that her sister has been kidnapped. In *Manhattan*, Isaac meets Mary.)

SEQUENCE B CD-2

The protagonist struggles to get to grips with the Call to Action crisis established at the end of Sequence A. But soon after there's another shock in store: a Big Event which signifies what they're up against. This is what the film's really about. The main conflict they'll have to tackle. From this they must make a Big Decision to embark on a new and potentially life-changing adventure. When they make this Decision we know they're committed to solving the crisis established at the Call to Action and Big Event, and this signals the end of Act One.

(Neo takes the red pill in *The Matrix_*and enters "the real world". In *American Pie*, the guys make a pact to lose their virginity.)

SEQUENCE C CD-3

The start of the strange and often scary new world in which the protagonist is often a "fish out of water". This sequence contains, what Blake Snyder calls, The Promise of the Premise: the trailer moments in which the hero struggles to adapt to the new world. Note that the end of this sequence doesn't determine the end of an act, but is still a definite step forward or backwards in the protagonist's main goal established at the end of Act One.

(Truman gets stuck on the bus and fails to leave the island in *The Truman Show*. Tor is humiliated by rival cheerleaders, The Clovers, in *Bring It On*.)

SEQUENCE D C D - 4

Having failed or succeeded at the end of the last sequence, the protagonist pushes on, invariably trying a different tactic in order to achieve their overall goal. The end of this sequence ends on either an "up" or a "down" and signals the script's Midpoint — usually a surprising twist of some kind. Here, the protagonist feels the full power of the antagonist but, conversely, is now fully committed to the goal, or a new variation of the goal. The stakes are raised as the protagonist turns a corner and a "new self" is born.

(In *Jaws*, Chief Brody realizes they've caught the wrong shark. Charles returns home to find killer, LaRoche, in his house chatting to his wife and kids in *Derailed*.)

SEQUENCE E CD 5

This sequence marks the beginning of the "changed hero". They begin to understand what they really want, but also to further realize the power of their adversary. The stakes are raised as they react to whatever new crisis occurred at the Midpoint. This is sometimes known as the "Gain" section of the script in which everything seems to be going well for the protagonist, but in reality it's not. For example, in Romantic Comedies this is often where the protagonist falls in love, but there is a sting in the tail at the end of the sequence in which love is hindered and the protagonist faces an unexpected setback.

(In *Boogie Nights*, Dirk rises to the top but becomes too cocky and gets fired. In *Sideways*, Miles finally gets his act together and goes to see Maya at the restaurant, but she's not working that night.)

SEQUENCE F —CD 6

The end of this sequence also corresponds to the end of Act Two, again either an "up" or "down" ending depending on the climax to the overall film. The end of Sequence F can be viewed as either a "false victory" or "false defeat." Either the hero seemingly wins the day in an "All Is Joy" moment, but it's a temporary victory, or they wind up in a worst place than at the start of the film with an "All Is Lost" moment, but it's a fleeting defeat. However, often in Horror, things reach a low point at the end of this sequence and then get even worse at the Climax.

(A high point is reached in the film *In Search of a Midnight Kiss*, when Wilson and Vivian kiss at midnight. A low point occurs in *The Blair Witch Project* when Heather makes a direct-to-camera apology to her parents realizing she's going to die.)

SEQUENCE G   CD-7

This is often the shortest sequence of the screenplay as it's all about motion and urgency. The protagonist has finally realized what needs to be done to crack the mystery/get the girl/catch the killer, etc. The climax to Sequence G often corresponds directly to the Climax to the whole film, wrapping up the A and B stories on either "up" or "down" beats, and tying up any loose ends.

In most instances the protagonist has learned a great lesson by the end of the movie. They are not the same person they were at the beginning of their journey. In fact, they have performed a complete U-turn and now want the exact opposite thing from what they wanted at the start.

In Action/Adventure the transformation is sometimes great (*Wanted*), and sometimes insignificant (*James Bond*). In Thrillers, the arc is usually minimal, and likewise in Horror where the protagonist's primary concern is escape and survival.

(In *The Godfather*, Michael becomes head of the family. Benjamin dies at the end of *The Curious Case of Benjamin Button*.)

SEQUENCE H

The composition of this sequence depends on how the previous one ended. If Sequence G ended with the Screenplay Climax, the movie's over, but if it ended with an All Is Lost/All Is Joy success or failure, then this sequence becomes in effect Sequence G: the protagonist's sprint to solve the screenplay's main goal before it's too late.

(In *The Heartbreak Kid* remake, there are eight sequences ending on Sequence H. Sequence G ends with an All Is Lost failure when Eddie fails to win back Miranda. An eighth

Sequence H then begins with him packing up and leaving town, before we jump a year and a half in time when Miranda turns up to provide the film's neat ending.)

HOW SEQUENCES ARE BROKEN DOWN INTO SEGMENTS

While you may have heard countless times to "throw obstacles in the way of the protagonist" and "stick them in a hole and then try and get them out of it", sequences provide a solid structure to this conflict making the conflict easier to write.

Rather than randomly throwing obstacles at your protagonist in-between free-floating plot points, sequences provide a series of "mini-movies", each with rising conflict and resolution for them to traverse. It follows, naturally, that each sequence has a beginning, middle, and end which can be viewed as individual "acts". We call these "segments" and they work in exactly the same way as regular acts in a screenplay.

SEGMENT I: Raises a dramatic question/crisis which the protagonist attempts to solve during the sequence.

SEGMENT II: A series of strategies are followed, ending with a final chosen ploy and/or event: either an "up" or a "down" moment.

SEGMENT III: This new strategy is followed and the sequence goal is either achieved or fails.

It is important to grasp how closely these segments enable sequences to match the structure of the overall screenplay by using these same six major beats:

INCITING INCIDENT
CALL TO ACTION
BIG EVENT DECISION
MIDPOINT
ALL IS LOST/JOY
CLIMAX

Let's take a closer look at the composition of these three segments:

SEGMENT I

The first segment starts with an Inciting Incident which shows the audience the protagonist's original goal: the direction they think they're heading in this sequence. However, a major obstacle — the Call to Action — swiftly kicks in, spinning the sequence in a new direction and setting a new goal for the protagonist to achieve by its end. A Sequence Big Event comes at the end of the segment and, like in the overall screenplay, is a continuation of the dramatic question/crisis raised at the Call to Action in which things get even better/worse.

Like the previous Inciting Incident and Call to Action, this can be either a positive or negative moment, but this one is usually the reverse of the Sequence Climax (found later in Segment III).

SEGMENT II

The second segment begins with the protagonist struggling to resolve the conflict established at the Sequence Big Event. But it's not long before they hit an unexpected twist — the Sequence Midpoint — usually an obstacle, or revelation, in which the stakes are raised, advancing or hindering the protagonist's chances of achieving their sequence goal.

The segment ends with either an All Is Lost or All Is Joy moment: an "up" or "down" event that pushes the protagonist into "Act III" of the sequence. This moment fools the audience into believing the sequence will end a certain way, either positively or negatively, but then the opposite happens at the Sequence Climax.

SEGMENT III

The strategy decided upon at the end of the last segment is played out here, culminating in the Sequence Climax: usually the opposite charge to that found at the Sequence Big Event.

For example, if the Sequence Big Event was a negative event (-), this Sequence Climax is usually a positive event (+). i.e. in the final sequence in *Bridesmaids*, Helen tells Annie Lillian's missing (-) All three women celebrate at the wedding (+).

THE SCENE AS A SEQUENCE

Another point to consider is that although in most cases these major plot points occur at the end of each scene, sometimes they occur within the same scene.

For example, in Sequence F in *Collateral*, Max speeds up while driving Vincent (call to action), crashes the car and

Vincent runs off before the cop arrives (big event), the cop sees the dead body in the trunk and arrests him (midpoint), Max sees Annie is next on Vincent's hit-list (all is lost), Max overpowers the cop and takes off after Vincent (climax).

BUT WHAT ABOUT JEAN LUC GODDARD?

WHY SCREENWRITING STRUCTURE METHODS ARE SOMETIMES CALLED "ANTI-CREATIVE"

Many aspiring screenwriters want to "break the mold" and write a film true to their "artistic vision". They argue "what's the point of calling yourself a writer if all you are doing is filling in the blanks on a numbered pre-determined list of events?" But the fact is these structure rules are there for a reason: they work. Sequences are a part of a structure that all good films adhere to. The technique of writing by sequences has been employed by professional writers since the golden age of Hollywood. In fact, that's how films were first written — using sequences — as they mimic the early twelve to fifteen minute reels movies were originally made on.

Ultimately, as "anti-creative" as it may appear, mastering sequences within the three act structure is essential to writing an entertaining script and, in turn, being enjoyed by a reader, being optioned and becoming a professional screenwriter.

That's because these semi-fixed structural reference points emulate a natural ebb and flow — an up and down in the fortunes of the hero — essential to maintaining audience attention and maximizing their emotional connection to the story. The beats that make up each sequence resonate on a subliminal level with the audience, and that's why they're replicated in most films from *Alien* to *Zoolander*.

The old adage applies of only being able to break the rules once you've mastered them. The New Wave and Neo-Realist auteurs only made anti-structural avant-garde films after mastering Hollywood techniques earlier in their career, much the same way as Picasso started out as a "traditional" artist.

Filmmakers like Sophia Coppola can afford to write a forty-four page screenplay and turn it into a ninety-seven minute movie (*Somewhere*) because she's already a success. She has a track record. Aspiring screenwriters don't. If you want to independently produce and finance a film without any of the structural conformities required by Hollywood you're free to do so of course, but for those looking to break into the spec market with a well written screenplay, you're 100 percent more likely to by utilizing sequences and the structural norms of screenwriting.

A NOTE ON GENRE

WHY THIS BOOK CONTAINS SEQUENCE BREAKDOWNS OF EACH OF THE TOP FIVE GENRES IN HOLLYWOOD TODAY

We've discussed structure but what's the other crucial element in crafting a successful screenplay? Yes, it's that old nugget, genre.

It is essential that a screenplay conforms to a genre, or sub-genre, or tries something new by mixing genres. Audiences want to know what type of film they are going to see. Hollywood wants to know what type of film they're going to buy so they can package it to a particular audience. And selling a screenplay involves writing a story which satisfies the requirements of its genre.

As of writing, the top five screenplay genre categories selling in Hollywood are:

ACTION/ADVENTURE
THRILLER
COMEDY
HORROR
DRAMA

As you can see, thanks to the biggest demographic of people who go to movie theaters (teenage boys) Action/Adventure scripts are what's hot right now.

Comedies are always popular and sell well, despite the Romantic Comedy's mini downturn at the moment. Horror is another steady seller — cheap, simple plotting, easy to shoot and highly recommended for first time writers. Drama, as ever, is a notoriously hard sell but shouldn't be overlooked. If your drama script doesn't actually get made you can always use it as a writing sample to get other writing gigs.

Sometimes sci-fi and westerns are classified as "genres," but technically these are sub-genres found within one of the five mentioned above. In this book we concentrate on these top five genres and break down one film from each into sequences.

THE FIXED, YET FLUID, NATURE OF SEQUENCES

We will be using the following symbols in the title of each sequence breakdown to denote whether it starts on a positive and ends on a negative, or vice-versa.

(+ / -) The overall sequence goes from a positive to a negative. The positive charge is the Big Event of the sequence at the end of its first segment. At the Sequence Climax, though, things will end badly for the protagonist.

(- / +) The reverse situation to the above. The overall sequence goes from a negative to a positive with the negative charge coming at the Big Event, and the positive at the Sequence Climax.

(+ / + +) Sometimes, instead of going from good to bad, a sequence will go from good to really good.

(- / - -) Similarly, sometimes a protagonist's fortunes within a sequence will go from bad to even worse.

It's worth bearing in mind, however, that these positive/ negative charges are not set in stone. The outlines broken down within this book are, of course, open to interpretation, and it's entirely possible that the original writer, you, or anyone else may disagree with certain elements to certain outlines. For example, does Sequence E in *Raiders of the Lost Ark* end when Indy's truck is hidden by the townspeople seconds before the Nazis arrive? Or when he and Marion kiss on the boat later that night?

Another example: we've seen a sequence breakdown of *Bridesmaids* online broken down into eight sequences instead of seven, with the end of the seventh sequence coming when Helen arrives at Annie's house asking for help finding Lillian. That's their interpretation, but not ours. (The end of a sequence marks the culmination of a conflict, not the beginning of one.)

Overall, the occasional difference of opinion over the placement of a scene in one sequence or another is inevitable. The important thing is that the rhythm of the sequence and its general beginning, middle and end are in the right place. The following films are presented chronologically and were chosen for being relatively modern, well known and excellent examples of their genre.

RAIDERS OF THE LOST ARK

Steven Spielberg, George Lucas and Lawrence Kasdan combined to bring us a 1930s adventure magazine-style romp in this, the first and best of the Indiana Jones series: *Raiders of the Lost Ark*. Sticking to genre convention, the opening sequence is an extended set-piece picking up at the tail end of the last adventure and unrelated to the main plot apart from introducing us to the rivalry between Indy and Belloq. This is specifically designed to hook the viewer with exciting action. In some ways, due to its length, this could be seen as a sequence in itself, but the main story doesn't kick in until the Call to Action when Indy hears about the Nazi's plans for the Ark. It's more of an extended scene than an actual sequence. The warnings from Marcus serve as a form of Refusal of the Call, but Indy's too excited to heed them and from here it's straight to Nepal. Here, Indy becomes entwined with his ex, Marion, throwing his plans out of sync — now he has a partner — wrapping up Sequence B and Act One.

The writers raise the stakes in the next sequence by making things personal when Indy believes Marion has been killed. Now the conflict not just about saving the world, but revenge. Giving the protagonist a personal motivation to their quest is important in Action/Adventure scripts to save the action from becoming too detached by simply showing one fight scene or explosion after another. The key to writing a good Action/ Adventure screenplay is reversals. The roller-coaster ride feel to *Raiders* is obtained through the following sequences in which the Ark constantly changes hands between Indy and the Nazis.

The Climax can be said to be the only possibly disappointing part of the film as Indy is saved, not only by a James Bond-like failure of the antagonists to just finish him off, but by a Deus Ex Machina moment when the power of the Ark wipes out the Nazis. But these are minor grievances — this is an essential screenplay and film to study for all those wishing to write Action/Adventure.

RAIDERS OF THE LOST ARK (1981)

SCREENPLAY BY LAWRENCE KASDAN/STORY BY GEORGE LUCAS & PHILIP KAUFMAN

ACT ONE
Sequence A – Indy is given the mission to find the Ark (- / +)

I

Super: South America, 1936.

Indiana Jones leads a team of explorers through a jungle. Several men flee in fear but Indy and the one remaining helper, Satipo, enter a cave.

Inside, Indy and Satipo have to traverse several obstacles such as tarantulas, traps, poisoned darts and a chasm. Satipo dies but Indy escapes with a golden statue. Outside, he finds himself face to face with arch nemesis, Belloq, and his band of Native American warriors.

Indy grabs an opportunity to run after handing over the statue. The natives give chase. Indy climbs onto his friend's plane and they take off.

Weeks later, Indy teaches an archaeology class in college. His friend, Marcus arrives after class and Indy tells him he can get the statue. He needs $2,000 to get to Marrakech. **(inciting incident)**

In the main hall, Marcus takes Indy to meet two guys from army intelligence. **(call to action)**

Indy realizes the Nazi's have discovered Tanis, the supposed resting place of the Lost Ark. **(negative big event / screenplay inciting incident)**

II
The Nazi's are now looking for the headpiece for the staff of Ra which is required to give the location of the Ark. **(midpoint)**

An army which carries the Ark before it is invincible. **(all is lost)**

III
At home, Indy celebrates with Marcus — the army intelligence guys want Indy to get to the ark before the Nazis. Indy says he has to find Ravenwood, his former Professor and

last man to see the headpiece. **(positive climax / screenplay call to action)**

Sequence B – Indy finds the headpiece (- / +)

I

Indy gets on a plane, watched by sinister Nazi agent, Toht. **(inciting incident)**

The plane flies to Nepal.

In a tavern, Indy's ex-girlfriend and Abner's daughter, Marion, beats a man in a drinking contest. Everyone leaves. Indy arrives and she punches him, still upset about their past. **(call to action / screenplay b-story)**

He needs the headpiece her father collected, but she's reluctant to help and says he's dead. Indy offers her $5,000. She tells him to come back tomorrow. **(negative big event)**

II

Indy leaves and Marion pulls the headpiece from around her neck... The Nazi, Toht, enters with his henchmen.

Marion tells him she doesn't have the headpiece, so he threatens to torture her. Indy bursts in and a shoot-out starts. **(midpoint)**

Toht accidentally burns an imprint of the headpiece on his hand. Marion saves Indy's life, they win the shoot-out and she grabs the headpiece. **(all is joy / screenplay big event)**

III

Outside, she shows Indy the headpiece and says now they're partners. **(positive climax / screenplay big decision)**

ACT TWO
Sequence C – Indy discovers the Ark's location (- / +)

I

Indy's plane flies to Cairo.

In Egypt, Indy and Marion meet Sallah who's worried about the power of the Ark. He tells Indy the Nazi's are close to discovering it using the burnt imprint on Toht's hand to create a replica of the headpiece. **(inciting incident)**

Indy and Marion walk through the town and Sallah's pet monkey disappears. It runs to a man with an eye-patch who then informs the Nazis. Suddenly, Indy and Marion are set upon by a group of Arab assassins. **(call to action)**

Marion hides in a basket. Indy looks for her in a sea of people with baskets. The Nazis put the basket on a truck and Indy shoots it causing it to blow up. **(negative big event)**

II

Indy sits depressed, drinking. The Nazis arrive and take him to meet Belloq who says they're the same and about the Ark being a transmitter to God. Indy is about to start a shootout when some kids come in and save him.

Outside, he meets Sallah who already knows Marion's dead.

The one-eyed man laces some dates with poison.

Sallah tells Indy Belloq has the headpiece and he's been given a new spot to dig with the Nazis: the Well of Souls. After talking to a Shaman, Indy realizes the Nazi's staff for the headpiece is too long: they're digging in the wrong place. **(midpoint)**

Indy and Sallah, dressed as workers, supervise a dig in the desert.

Indy enters the map room. He places the headpiece on the staff. A bright light shines across the floor illuminating the location of the Ark. **(all is joy)**

III

Outside, Indy finds Marion tied up in a tent — the Nazis must've switched baskets. Indy realizes he can't let her go because they'll know she's gone. He leaves her there saying he'll be back.

Indy looks through a telescope at the location of the Ark. **(positive climax / screenplay big decision success)**

Sequence D – The Nazis capture the Ark (+ / -)

I

Belloq talks to the Nazis who think Marion knows the Ark's location. Toht, with a burnt hand, arrives to question her.
Indy, Sallah and some men start digging in the desert. **(inciting incident)**

That night, they dig and find a secret chamber -- the Well of Souls. **(call to action)**

Meanwhile, Belloq gives Marion food and water. He makes her put on a beautiful white dress. He says he can protect her from the Nazis if she tells him all she knows.

Indy enters the chamber and sets the snakes on fire. **(positive big event)**

II

Marion flirts with Belloq, encouraging him to drink.

Indy and Sallah find the Ark. **(midpoint)**

Marion and Belloq get drunk and she pulls a knife on him. She's stopped at the door by the Nazis.

Indy and Sallah box up the Ark and take it back up to the surface. **(all is joy)**

Belloq and the Nazis see Indy and the others with the Ark in the distance. The Nazis rush over.

Belloq taunts Indy from outside — they're going to take the Ark to Berlin. They throw Marion down with him and seal up the opening.

III

Indy and Marion try to fend off the snakes. Indy sees snakes coming through the walls. He crashes through it using a monument. They find daylight. **(negative climax / screenplay midpoint)**

Sequence E – Indy recaptures the Ark (- / +)

I

Indy and Marion climb outside. They see the plane the Nazi's are going to fly the Ark out with. **(inciting incident)**

Indy gets into a fist fight with a huge Nazi. Belloq and the Nazis see explosions in the distance. Oil spreads, threatening to blow up the plane. Indy gets Marion out and they escape the plane just before it blows. Belloq realizes it's Indy. **(call to action)**

Sallah meets Indy and Marion. He tells them the Ark's on a truck bound for Cairo. **(negative big event)**

II

Indy watches the Ark being loaded. Belloq and the Nazis drive off with it.

Indy takes off on horseback after the truck. **(midpoint)**

He climbs onboard and takes it over. A Nazi climbs aboard and fights Indy. Indy manages to overpower him and drive Belloq off the road. **(all is joy)**

III

Indy arrives back in town and the locals hide the truck before Belloq and the Nazis get there. **(positive climax / screenplay midpoint success)**

Sequence F – The Nazis get back the Ark & capture Marion (+ / -)

I

Indy and Marion say goodbye to Sallah and board a boat. **(inciting incident)**

Onboard, Marion tends to Indy's wounds. They kiss.

The next morning, Indy goes on deck to find the Nazis boarding the ship. They take Marion and the Ark. Indy hides and the captain says he killed Indy. Belloq takes Marion. **(call to action)**

Indy climbs on board the Nazi sub nearby to cheering crowds on the ship. **(positive big event)**

II

On board the sub, Indy beats up a Nazi and takes his uniform. Belloq says he wants to open the Ark before they get to Berlin. **(midpoint)**

The Nazis walk with the Ark through the desert. Indy appears with a bazooka threatening to blow up the Ark if they don't give him Marion. Belloq calls his bluff, telling him to blow it up. **(all is lost)**

III

Indy crumbles and they arrest him. **(negative climax / screenplay all is lost)**

ACT THREE
Sequence G – The Ark kills the Nazis (- / +)

I

The Nazis prepare to open the Ark with Indy and Marion looking on, tied to a post. **(inciting incident)**

Belloq opens it to find it is filled with sand. **(call to action)**

A strange electrical storm comes out of the Ark. **(negative big event)**

II

Ghost-like figures begin swooping around the room. Indy tells Marion to keep her eyes shut no matter what. **(midpoint)**

The Nazis are killed by the ghosts whirling around them in a rampaging fire. When Indy and Marion open their eyes, the place is deserted. **(all is joy / screenplay climax)**

III

In Washington, Indy is congratulated by the army guys. Indy and Marcus are angry they won't tell them where the Ark is. He says they have "top men" working on it.

Outside, Marion offers to buy Indy a drink. They leave arm in arm. **(b-story climax)**

The Ark is padlocked up and put in storage among hundreds of other boxes containing top secret contents. **(screenplay dénouement)**

BRIDESMAIDS

Penned by SNL star Kristen Wiig and Annie Mumolo this was the movie that brought the female-driven comedy bang up to date. While much of the humor may not be to everybody's taste, veering as it does into producer Judd Apatow's favorite comedy weapon — farts and feces — there's an emotional core to the film that elevates it above your average gross out comedy.

Some people like to call *Bridesmaids* a Romantic Comedy, but it's not. The core conflict/relationship and A-story is between Annie and Lillian. Annie's relationship with the cop, Rhodes, is the B-story — the thing that helps Annie realize what she needs to change within herself to resolve the A-story.

Likewise, all of the sequence climaxes revolve around the A-story dilemma: will Annie be able to manage her rivalry with Helen and successfully complete her maid-of-honor duties?

At the end of Sequence B, note the introduction of the B-story on Annie's way back from meeting Helen for the first time and realizing she's a rival. The B-story is Annie's relationship with Rhodes and the writers cleverly tie this in to the main plot by making her meet him due to her upset state of mind — she's annoyed about Helen and so she's swerving all over the road as she drives, and he's a traffic cop… They could've made Rhodes a new neighbor or something and she meets him the next day, but it's always a good idea to make things happen because of something else that's just happened. Cause and effect.

From here, many of the sequences merely represent each stage in a maid-of-honor's run up to a real life wedding. Annie has to organize the dress fitting (sequence C), the girls go on the bachelorette party (sequence D), the wedding shower (sequence F), the wedding itself (sequence G). The writers have simply stuck to obvious real-life circumstances for inspiration. Kristen and Annie wanted to write about a story about maid-of-honor conflicts and so they based all of the sequences and set-pieces around maid-of-honor duties. Simple.

Of course, writing a Comedy screenplay as good as Bridesmaids isn't simple at all, but it can be made easier by just sticking to the stages and processes of whatever event you may be writing about.

BRIDESMAIDS (2011)
SCREENPLAY BY KRISTEN WIIG & ANNIE MUMOLO

ACT ONE
Sequence A – Lillian asks Annie to be her Maid of Honor (- / +)

I

Annie has awkward sex with Ted at her house. It's clear she's way more into him than he is into her. (inciting incident / screenplay inciting incident)

The next morning, Annie does herself up in the mirror and sneaks back into Ted's bed. He says he doesn't want a relationship and tells her to leave. (call to action)

Outside, she can't get out the high gate, so she starts to climb over but it opens as she's halfway across — a car is waiting to get in. (negative big event)

II

In a park, Annie works out with her friend, Lillian, near a workout class. The instructor calls them freeloaders and tells them to get lost.

In a cafe, Annie and Lillian discuss Lillian's relationship with Doug. Annie defends herself for having sex with Ted. Lillian says she should stop it because he's an asshole.

They walk to work and on the way stop outside her failed bakery store... **(midpoint)**

Annie works in a jewelers. She offends an Asian couple and they leave. Her boss reprimands her and brings over another worker to show her how it's done. Her boss tells her she only got the job because of her mom.

At home, Annie's flatmate, Brynn, talks about tattoos. Her brother, Gil, arrives and asks her about the rent. Annie tells him she'll have it soon. **(all is lost)**

III

Annie arrives at Lillian's who tells her she's engaged. Yay! She asks Annie to be her maid of honor. **(positive climax / screenplay call to action)**

Annie lies in bed thinking…

Sequence B – Annie realizes Helen's a rival (+ / -)

I

Annie arrives at her mom's to take her to the engagement party. Her mom says she can't go anymore because she's going to AA, even though she's never had a drink. Her mom gives her advice and asks if she wants to move in with her. **(inciting incident)**

Annie arrives at the party in her beat up car. **(call to action)**

She goes inside a big house and meets Lillian who introduces her to Rita who talks about her two kids. Then, Annie meets Becca and Kevin, irritating newlyweds who mistake a man standing near her as her boyfriend. Doug's inappropriate sister, Megan, tells a weird story. Annie meets Helen, a stuck up woman who's married to Doug's boss. **(positive big event)**

II

Later, Lillian's dad makes a speech. He hands over to Annie who makes a short, but sweet, speech. Helen makes a big speech about friendship. Not wanting to be out-done Annie makes another speech, this time about friendship. The rivalry has already started — both Helen and Annie want the last word on the speech. **(midpoint)**

Later, Annie talks crap about Helen to Lillian who says she should hang out with Helen as a favor. **(negative climax / screenplay big event)**

III

Annie drives home complaining to herself about Helen and swerving all over the road. She gets pulled by a cop, Rhodes. She proves she's not drunk but he gives her a ticket for not having a tail light. He remembers her cake shop and her ex and lets her off the ticket as long as she gets the light fixed. **(b-story)**

Montage: At home, Annie looks at stuff about her cake shop. She bakes a cake and eats it. She thinks…

ACT TWO

Sequence C – Annie messes up the dress-fitting (+ / -)

I

At a tennis court, Helen tells Annie people change, but Annie says they stay the same. Helen's step-kids arrive. They're rude to her and leave. **(inciting incident)**

Later, Annie and Helen play tennis doubles. It's very competitive and escalates into deliberately hitting each other in the body with tennis balls.

At home, Annie says Brynn needs to pay rent. Brynn confesses she read Annie's journal.

Annie takes Lillian and the bridesmaids to a Mexican restaurant. Judging from the exterior, they're not impressed.

Inside, Annie tells them about the wedding shower: French themed. Helen says they should think about it. They come up with suggestions. **(call to action)**

Annie takes to the girls to a dress shop, but can't get in. Helen gets them in. **(positive big event)**

II

Inside, they check out the dresses. Helen wants a $800 dress. Lillian says a major designer has done her wedding dress.

Later, they wear the dresses, still trying to decide, but soon they all start to feel ill. **(midpoint)**

Lillian arrives, wearing the wedding dress. Everyone rushes to the bathroom, but Helen's fine. Annie also says she feels fine. **(all is lost)**

III

Lillian rushes outside but can't make it to the bathroom in time and poops in the road. **(negative climax / screenplay big decision failure)**

Annie drives a shell-shocked Lillian home.

Sequence D – Annie ruins the Vegas trip & loses Maid of Honor duties (+ / -)

I

Annie lies in bed with Ted. She invites him to the wedding, but he doesn't want to go. She says she'll take a guy called "George" she just made up.

Annie runs into Rhodes at the gas station. **(inciting incident)**

They sit on his car, chatting about weddings. He tells her to set up a new bakery. She says she could be a cop.

Later, he teaches her to read license plates by the side of the road. They chase after a speeding car.

Annie send the girls an email about the bachelorette party. **(call to action)**

She receives a call from Helen straight away about using a lake house. Rita calls and suggests Vegas. Becca calls about Vegas. Megan calls… it's Vegas. Turns out Helen has already called everyone. **(positive big event)**

The girls walk in slo-mo to the plane.

II

On the plane, Helen tells Lillian that Annie refused to fly first class with them.

Annie gets nervous, sitting next to another nervous flyer. Annie comes up to Lillian and Helen who gives her a sleeping pill. Rita can't believe Becca hasn't been with anyone but her husband. Megan talks to a guy who she thinks is an Air Marshall. Helen joins Annie who gives her a Scotch. Annie appears in first class, drunk. She argues with the steward and leaves. **(midpoint)**

Later, Annie appears in first class again. The steward throws her out again. Megan flirts with the guy in her seat. Becca and Rita get drunk. Annie sees something on the wing and freaks out. Everyone freaks out.

They land in Wyoming and are escorted off the plane. **(all is lost)**

III

They sit on a bus. Annie apologizes to Lillian who says she's giving the maid of honor responsibility to Helen. Annie's sad, but agrees. **(negative climax / screenplay midpoint)**

Sequence E – Annie loses Rhodes, gets fired, moves in with her mom (+ / -)

I

Annie drives and spots Rhodes in his car. **(inciting incident)**

They talk in a bar about her screw up. He says she should open the bakery again. He says he's been thinking about her. **(call to action)**

They burst into his house, kissing. **(positive big event)**

II

Next morning, Annie wakes up to find Rhodes smiling at her. She's a bit unnerved and so he goes to the kitchen.

Later, Annie joins Rhodes to find he's set up a mini-bakery for her. He wants to reignite her passion for baking. She's not impressed and leaves, saying he doesn't know her and that last night was a mistake. **(midpoint)**

Annie drives and leaves a message for Lillian about running out on Rhodes.

Brynn wakes Annie up — a package has arrived for her.

Annie opens Helen's wedding shower invite.

At work, a girl comes in asking for a BFF bracelet. Annie is rude to her and they argue.

Annie is fired. She collects her stuff and leaves.

Annie listens to a voice mail from Rhodes saying he won't bother her anymore. **(all is lost / screenplay midpoint failure)**

III

Gil and Brynn tell Annie they're kicking her out the apartment.

Annie moves into her mom's. **(negative climax)**

Annie looks at her old store.

Sequence F – Annie falls out with Lillian (+ / -)

I

Annie drives down a long driveway to Helen's house. **(inciting incident)**

She is escorted on a horse up to the massive house and enters. **(call to action)**

In the garden, she meets Lillian who says everything's okay. **(positive big event)**

II

Later, Lillian opens her presents. Annie made her a montage of photos and all her favorite stuff. Helen outdoes her by giving Lillian tickets to Paris. Everyone claps. Annie's jealous and freaks out, calling Helen a lesbian. **(midpoint)**

Annie says this isn't the Lillian she knows. Annie goes outside and destroys the huge wedding cookie. Lillian tells her not to come to the wedding and Annie leaves. **(all is lost / screenplay all is lost)**

III

Annie drives down the freeway. Megan drives up beside her and causes her to pull over. By the side of the road, a car runs into Annie's car, but drives on. Her car won't start.

Later, Annie receives a lecture by the side of the road from Rhodes about her tail-light. He says she just left after making him think she liked him. Ted pulls up in his car and Rhodes drives off.

Later, Ted drives Annie home. He says she can give him a blow-job if she wants. She tells him to pull over, gets out and walks. **(negative climax)**

ACT THREE
Sequence G – Annie and Lillian make up and Lillian gets married (- / +)

I

At home, Annie watches *Castaway*, crying. Megan arrives with a pack of puppies and tries to give her a pep talk. She pushes Annie around, telling her to fight for her life. Megan tells her life her story. They hug. **(inciting incident)**

Montage: Annie bakes. She introduces her mom to Bill. She leaves an "I'm Sorry" cake for Rhodes but he doesn't take it. She drives past again and sees it's being eaten by raccoons.

Annie's mom enters asking about Lillian's wedding. Annie's not going. **(call to action)**

Later, Annie opens the door to Helen who tells her Lillian's missing. **(negative big event)**

II

They drive. Helen apologizes to Annie and cries about not having any friends.

Annie stops at Rhodes' car parked by the side of the road. She asks for his help but he doesn't listen.

Montage: Annie goofs around driving past Rhodes to try and make him laugh and change his mind. Finally, he gives in.

Rhodes traces Lillian's cell to... her apartment. Annie apologizes. He says goodbye. **(midpoint)**

Annie and Helen arrive at Lillian's and Annie goes in alone. She finds Lillian in her bed. Lillian says it's been hard to do the wedding without her. They both apologize. **(positive climax / screenplay climax)**

III

Later, Annie laughs at Lillian's dress.

The wedding: Lillian gets married. Annie looks on. Helen introduces the band Wilson Phillips. Everyone dances. **(screenplay dénouement)**

Later, Lillian leaves with her husband. Megan tells Annie her prank. Helen arrives and Annie says they should hang out. They hug. Rhodes arrives. They kiss. He has to leave on a call and she goes with him. **(b-story climax)**

THE VIRGIN SUICIDES

Full of atmosphere and with a great soundtrack, *The Virgin Suicides* is a remarkably assured coming-of-age-drama and first feature from writer/director Sophia Coppola.

In a classic drama convention, the film explores the power struggle that occurs between the young and a rigid, unsympathetic social order: five blonde teenage girls sheltered from the world by their authoritarian parents in a Michigan suburb during the 1970s.

Witnessing their gradual descent are four local boys who become obsessed with the girls but never quite manage to figure them out. The film starts with a major change in the lives of the Lisbon's and, indeed, the neighborhood boys: Cecilia's suicide attempt which is a foreshadowing of the tragedy to come.

First, though, there is cause for optimism when Cecilia's suicide attempt causes a positive reaction from the parents at the end of Sequence A, and they are allowed more freedom. However, with Cecilia's suicide at the end of Sequence B and

Act One, the Lisbon's world is thrown out of control and the conditions are set for the girls' demise.

Lux soon takes over the film's focus as she embarks on a brief relationship with local heartthrob Trip Fontaine. The "Innermost Cave" (antagonist's lair) at the Midpoint is Trip's car in which the two frustrated lovers enjoy a passionate kiss. By entering his world, Lux knocks over the first domino that will culminate in all the girls' suicides.

The Gain section in Sequence E revolves around Trip and his friends taking the Lisbon girls to the school dance, but by the end of the next sequence Lux has missed curfew incurring the wrath of her mother.

Total lockdown dominates the rest of the girls' short lives and they leave the world — their neighborhood, parents and the boys — with an elusive mystery no-one will ever solve.

THE VIRGIN SUICIDES (1999)

SCREENPLAY BY SOFIA COPPOLA/BASED ON THE NOVEL BY JEFFREY EUGENIDES

ACT ONE

Sequence A – The Lisbon girls are allowed more freedom (- / +)

I

Scenes of quiet suburbia. A tree is posted by a worker with a sign for removal.

In a bathtub, Cecilia lies in her own blood. **(inciting incident / screenplay inciting incident)**

Mrs. Lisbon and curious neighbors watch as she's taken away in an ambulance. **(call to action)**

In hospital, Cecilia tells the doctor "what does he know?" — he's never been a 13-year-old girl. **(negative big event)**

II

Super: Michigan. 25 Years Ago.

A narrator describes how as teenagers they tried to put the pieces together about the Lisbon girls. The four boys — Chase, Parkie, Kevin, Tim — watch the Lisbon's arrive home with their five daughters: Cecilia, Lux, Bonnie, Mary and Therese. **(midpoint)**

The boys listen to a story from Paul Baldino about how he found Cecilia after her suicide attempt.

Neighbors gossip about Cecilia.

The boys say another love struck kid, Dominic, was to blame. Dominic watches Diana play tennis. When she left town he jumped off the roof of his relative's house.

A psychiatrist shows Cecilia some images.

He tells the Lisbons her act was a cry for help and says she needs a social outlet outside of school. **(all is joy / screenplay call to action)**

III

The Lisbons drive home.

The Lisbons eat dinner. A kid from school, Peter dines with them, awkward being surrounded by so many girls. Lux embarrasses him further by playing footsie with him.

Later, Peter goes upstairs to use the restroom in Cecilia's room. He looks around. He daydreams about Lux, but she suddenly enters and he flees the house. **(positive climax)**

Sequence B – Cecilia commits suicide (+ / -)

I

Lux sunbathes in her swimsuit. The narrator says from that day on things began to change… **(inciting incident)**

The narrator tells us how Mr. Lisbon was persuaded to throw the first and only party of their short lives. **(call to action)**

The girls excitedly get ready. **(positive big event)**

II

The boys enter and go down to the party in the basement. Cecilia sits looking bored. They all sit separately, nervous. Cecilia goes upstairs and moments later, there's a thud and a scream… **(midpoint)**

Everyone goes outside to find Cecilia's killed herself by jumping out the window. Mr Lisbon lifts her off the spiked fence. The boys leave, stunned. **(all is lost / screenplay big event)**

III

The Lisbon's funeral procession drives and meets a demonstration in the road. Mr Lisbon talks to them and they let him through.

At home, Mr Lisbon talks to the priest like nothing's happened. He says Mrs Lisbon won't come down. The priest goes upstairs to find the girls all together, silent. He tells Mrs Lisbon he listed her death as an accident. **(negative climax / screenplay big decision)**

ACT TWO
Sequence C – The boys try to grow closer to the girls (+ / -)

I

Neighbors watch men remove the iron fence Cecilia died on. **(inciting incident)**

The boys read in Cecilia's diary how Lux lusted after the garbage man. **(call to action)**

Montage: the girls in happier times. The narrator says the boys started to understand the girls. **(positive big event)**

II

A TV reporter knocks on the Lisbon's door to ask Therese and Mary about Cecilia. Mrs Lisbon slams the door in her face.

Neighbors watch Lydia Perl's news report.

That night, Mr Lisbon sees Cecilia in her room.

Tim wakes up and sees Cecilia at the end of his bed.

Chase sees Cecilia sitting in a tree.

The boys arrive at school. The girls arrive like nothing had happened. **(midpoint)**

Mr Lisbon teaches the boys.

Chase tries to talk to Mary at the locker.

In class, a girl talks about death in front of Bonnie and then apologizes.

The Lisbon girls hang out in silence in the restroom. **(all is lost)**

III
A teacher talks to the school about suicide rates. The narrator talks about the signs of suicide they were supposed to look out for as a class photo is taken.

Chase tries to talk to Mary again but she says he doesn't have to talk to her. **(negative climax / screenplay big decision failure)**

Sequence D – Trip gets together with Lux (- / +)

I
Tim watches a boy make Lux laugh — he can't believe it. **(b-story)**

Several schoolboys talk to the camera about their relationships with Lux. But the narrator says the only boy who got to know her was Trip Fontaine… **(inciting incident)**

Montage: Trip flirts with a girl. He walks down the hall and all the girls stare at him. He lets a girl into his house. He flirts in class.

The narrator says Trip could have any girl he wanted, but fell in love with Lux. Trip goes into the wrong class to avoid a teacher and ends up behind Lux. She smiles. **(call to action)**

Adult Trip talks to the camera about how he never got over Lux.

Lux ignores Trip at school. **(negative big event)**

II

Trip approaches the Lisbon girls outside, but Lux ignores him.

Trip sits depressed at home as his dad tries to advise him about Lux.

In the school movie theatre, Trip sits next to Lux as everyone watches a documentary. They silently flirt, then Trip says he's going to come round her house and ask her out. He leaves. **(midpoint)**

At the Lisbon's, Trip sits with the family watching TV.

Later, Trip says goodbye to Lux and leaves. **(all is lost)**

III

He gets in his car, disappointed. Lux suddenly jumps in the car and they passionately make out. She rushes back inside. **(positive climax / screenplay midpoint)**

Sequence E – The Lisbon girls are shut off from the world (+ / -)

I

At school, Trip asks Mr Lisbon if he can take Lux to homecoming dance. He says he'll see what he can do. **(inciting incident)**

At home, Mr Lisbon asks Mrs Lisbon about the dance. The girls are excited. **(call to action)**

At school, Mr Lisbon tells Trip he can take Lux. **(positive big event)**

II

On the football field, boys argue with Trip over who accompanies him and the other Lisbon girls to the dance.

At home, the girls ask Mr Lisbon who's going.

The girls and Mrs Lisbon shop for materials.

Mr Lisbon takes a photo of them.

The boys arrive at the Lisbon's and meet the girls. They all leave together.
In the car, the girls gossip about the neighbors.

Later, they smoke in the car.

At the dance, Trip and Lux hide and drink peach schnapps. They kiss.

They're announced homecoming king and queen. Everyone dances.

Later, Trip takes Lux outside for a walk. They arrive on the football field. **(midpoint)**

The guys and the Lisbon girls wait for Lux in the car. Finally, they leave.

Meanwhile, Trip and Lux make out on the field.

The boys drop the girls home.

Trip wakes up at dawn on the field with Lux beside him.

Later, Lux wakes up alone in the field. She leaves. **(all is lost)**

III

Lux arrives home in a cab. Mrs Lisbon angrily drags her inside.

Adult Trip tells us he liked Lux, but he didn't care how she got home that night. He says that was the last time he saw her.

The narrator says Mrs. Lisbon cracked down on the girls putting them under maximum security isolation and taking them out of school. The girls sit in their room, bored. **(negative climax / screenplay midpoint failure)**

Sequence F – The Lisbon girls commit suicide (+ / -)

I

Mrs. Lisbon makes Lux destroy her record collection. **(inciting incident)**

The girls watch the tree being cut down in their yard.

The boys watch Lux through a telescope making love on the roof. **(call to action)**

The boys listen to a guy tell a story about sleeping with Lux.

They watch Lux again.

At school, Mr. Lisbon is questioned by another teacher about the girls not being in school but he ignores him.

The tree surgeons want to cut down the Lisbon tree but the girls block them. They're forced to leave. A news crew arrives and the girls leave. **(positive big event)**

II

The girls hang out in their room. The narrator says Lux never spoke to Trip again. **(b-story climax)**

Therese collects travel catalogues and takes them inside. The boys read the same catalogues and imagine they travel with them. The narrator says this was the only way they could feel close to the girls. But they were slipping away…

The boys decipher Morse Code from the girls. **(midpoint)**

The boys find cards from the girls asking for help.

They call the girls on the phone and play a song down the line. The girls respond with another song.

Tim finds a note from the girls telling them to wait for their signal at midnight. **(all is joy)**

III
That night, they see the signal and go over to the house. Lux meets them and they agree to go driving somewhere. She lets them in, then leaves to wait in the car. The boys hear a noise and find one of them hanging. Another is dead in the kitchen… **(negative climax / screenplay all is lost)**

ACT THREE
Sequence G – The boys fail to understand the Lisbon girls (- / - -)

I
The next morning, the bodies are taken away. **(inciting incident)**

The narrator describes what must have been the sequence of events that night. The cops find Lux dead in the garage.

News reports on the deaths.

Mr and Mrs Lisbon leave the house for good. Mrs. Lisbon says none of the daughters lacked any love. **(call to action)**

The narrator says after the suicides they sold what they could and left the house. The boys only had pieces of the puzzle... **(negative big event)**

II

The boys' parents' lives return to normal. **(midpoint)**

At a themed party the boys mingle and the narrator says they hoped to forget about the Lisbon girls. **(all is lost)**

III

The next day, the boys stare at the empty Lisbon house — as the narrator says the girls hadn't heard them calling, and they would never find the pieces to put them back together. **(negative climax / screenplay climax)**

THRILLER BREAKDOWN

COLLATERAL

Stuart Beattie narrowly missed out on a Bafta Best Screenplay award for this stylish thriller directed by Michael Mann.

Max is the classic Thriller stooge — an ordinary man who finds himself involved in an extraordinary situation — when he is forced to drive contract killer, Vincent, from hit to hit. Unlike in a Romantic Comedy, Max's life is not changed in any way when he first meets Vincent. Therefore, the change, and the Call to Action, occurs when a dead body falls from the sky slamming onto his cab's hood. As is convention, Sequence B is shorter than Sequence A. We've had the long set-up and crisis that spins the protagonist's life out of sync. Now we need to get straight to what he's going to do about it. Max's only hope is to try and attract the attention of a passer-by while Vincent is inside carrying out a hit. With a nice touch of irony, though, these passers-by turn out to be thieves.

Vincent's killing of the thugs also signals the death knell for Vincent's chances of escape. He is now locked together with Vincent and dragged into the upside down world of Act Two... What Max thought would be a good idea in throwing away Vincent's hit list, only creates further problems and leads to the classic negative twist at the Midpoint in which he becomes mistaken by the cops for Vincent and the stakes are raised even higher. The Gain section in Sequence E is Fanning realizing Max is not Vincent, but again, this reverses and we end on a negative when Fanning's shot by Vincent. The next sequence nearly ends on "up" when Vincent flees, but reverses once more when Max realizes who Vincent's next hit is. Having taken on some of the attributes of the antagonist, Max takes matters into his own hands and gives chase. He's no longer an ordinary guy.

COLLATERAL (2004)
SCREENPLAY BY STUART BEATTIE

ACT ONE
Sequence A – Max realizes Vincent's a killer (+ / -)

I

Vincent walks through LAX airport terminal. A man bumps into him and they switch bags. **(inciting incident / screenplay inciting incident)**

Max gets into his cab and drives out the cab station. On the road he listens to an arguing couple in the back.

At the airport, he picks up a business woman, Annie. They flirt and make a bet that the ride will be free if his route's slower than hers. **(b-story)**

Later, she admits she was wrong and they chat and flirt some more. He says he's just driving part time and is starting a limo business. He clocks that she's a lawyer. She talks about her job and insecurities. They say goodbye and she gets out the cab. But then she comes back and gives him her number.
Vincent heads upstairs in an office building. He passes Annie. Outside, he gets in Max's cab. They drive and Vincent asks

Max about his life. Vincent asks Max to hang with him for the night.He offers $600, but Max says it's against regulations. **(call to action)**

Finally, they agree. Max parks around the corner. **(positive big event)**

II

Vincent heads inside. As Max eats in his cab, a dead body crashes onto the windshield. **(midpoint)**

Max freaks out and Vincent forces him to help put the guy in the trunk. Vincent makes Max drive. **(negative climax / screenplay call to action)**

III

Detective Fanning enters the room of the dead guy, Ramone, looking for him. He sees the open window and, putting two and two together, calls base.

Sequence B – Vincent traps Max (- / - -)

I

Max drives Vincent, saying he's not up for it, but Vincent tells him not to worry about "one fat guy." **(inciting incident)**

A cop pulls them over. Vincent is about to shoot them when they get called away on another job.

Vincent makes Max stop for another hit. He ties Max to the wheel. **(call to action)**

Base calls in and says Max will have to pay for the damage to the cab. Vincent tells them to stick the job. He makes Max stand up to his boss and leaves. **(negative big event)**

II

A man answers the door to his apartment. It's Vincent... **(midpoint)**

Max tries to get people's attention by sounding the horn. Some guys arrive but they rob him and take the case. **(all is lost / screenplay big event)**

III

Vincent arrives and shoots them both dead. **(negative climax / screenplay big decision)**

ACT TWO
Sequence C – Max stands up to Vincent (- / +)

I

At a gas station, Max fills up. Vincent says they're ahead of schedule so he'll buy him a drink at a jazz club. **(inciting incident)**

Fanning tells his colleagues the case is his. A cop says there was a cab there earlier. Fanning tries to work out what happened.

At the jazz club, Vincent arranges to talk to the trumpet player/owner of the club. **(call to action)**

Later, Max and Vincent talk to the owner about his experience playing with Miles Davis. The owner realizes who Vincent is. Vincent shoots him dead. **(negative big event)**

II

Outside, Vincent catches up with Max and punches him. The boss calls again and Vincent realizes Max's due to see his mom. It will break the routine and draw attention to them so Vincent wants to go see her. **(midpoint)**

At the hospital, they get in an elevator with Fanning. They get out and Fanning goes up to level five.

Max and Vincent arrive in his mom's room. He introduces her to Vincent who's charming as hell. Max's mom tells Vincent her son is a limo driver. Max flees with the case. Vincent chases after him.

On a bridge Max stops. He throws the case over onto the freeway. **(positive climax / screenplay big event success)**

III

Fanning looks at bodies in a morgue. The mortician tells him there's a pattern in the gunshot wounds between Fanning's guy, Ramone, and the two thugs who robbed Max.

Fanning calls his colleague and says the lawyer turned criminal who represented Ramone — Sylvester Clarke — is dead.

Sequence D – The cops think Max is Vincent (- / - -)

I

Max drives Vincent to the next hit. Vincent mocks him about lying to his mom. Vincent talks about his tough upbringing. Max talks about his limo business. **(inciting incident)**

They stop. Vincent tells Max he has to go in and ask for Felix who's connected to the guy who hired him. He has to pretend to be him and get the list of hits from him. **(call to action)**

Vincent says he has ten minutes or he drives off and kills his mom on the way out of town. **(negative big event)**

II

Max is searched before going in. Frank and his guys watch him on CCTV. Security finally let Max in.

Fanning and his colleague arrive and ask Frank if he's seen anything. Fanning notices the CCTV and Max's cab. He sees the smashed windshield… **(midpoint)**

Inside the club, Max meets Felix who gets angry that he lost the list. Max takes on Vincent's persona and gets away with it. **(all is joy)**

III

The cops listen in to the conversation and using voice recognition pick up the name "Vincent". **(negative climax / screenplay midpoint)**

Max leaves. Felix tells his bodyguard to follow him, and if anything goes wrong to kill him.

Sequence E – Vincent shoots Fanning (+ / -)

I

Max gets back in the cab and gives Vincent the flash drive. They leave. **(inciting incident)**

The cops see this and leave to start the operation on Max and his cab. Fanning doesn't think Max is Vincent. **(call to action)**

The cops give chase. **(positive big event)**

II

Vincent tells Max to call Annie. They arrive at the club. The cops follow.

Vincent kills a guy in the crowd. Frank sees Max and tells him to get his hands in the air. A shootout. Chaos. **(midpoint)**

The target flees. Vincent saves Max's life. Fanning grabs Max — he knows he's not Vincent. **(all is joy)**

III

Fanning gets Max outside but Vincent shoots Fanning dead. He makes Max drive off. **(negative climax / screenplay midpoint failure)**

Sequence F – Max realizes Annie's next on the hit list (+ / -)

I

Vincent and Max argue about killing Fanning and others who he doesn't even know. **(inciting incident)**

Vincent taunts Max about his "sad" life and how he hasn't done what he said he'd do. Max speeds up. **(call to action)**

Max drives straight through red lights. Vincent puts a gun to his head telling him to slow down. Max deliberately crashes the car. Vincent climbs out the wreckage and runs off before the cops arrive. **(positive big event)**

II
The cop asks Max if he's okay, but then see the dead body and arrest him. **(midpoint)**

Max sees Annie is Vincent's next hit. **(all is lost)**

III
Max overpowers the cop and ties him to the cab. He runs off after Vincent. **(negative climax / screenplay all is lost)**

ACT THREE
Sequence G – Vincent dies (- / +)

I

Max steals a guy's cell phone and tries to call Annie but there's no signal. He runs though a parking lot. **(inciting incident)**

Vincent enters Annie's building. She's working late in her office. Max calls her and tries to explain about Felix hiring Vincent to kill witnesses. **(call to action)**

Vincent bursts into her office but she's not there, she's in another office. Max sees Vincent in the building. He tries to warn her but his battery runs out. **(negative big event)**

II

Max runs. Annie calls the cops. Vincent smashes the electricity lines. Max arrives at the building. The lights go out. Annie sees Vincent and hides. Max smashes his way in.

Vincent hunts Annie in the dark. Max appears and shoots Vincent but he's not dead. He chases after Max and Annie. **(midpoint)**

They run onto the subway and sneak onto a train.

Vincent climbs on from the back. He hunts them through the carriage. **(all is lost)**

III

He finds them and shoots but runs out of ammo. He sits down. Max sits opposite. Vincent dies. **(positive climax / screenplay climax)**

Max and Annie get off the train, finally safe. **(b-story climax)**

HORROR BREAKDOWN

WOLF CREEK

"WHY ARE YOU DOING THIS TO ME?!" Whether it's a demon, a zombie, a ghost or, in this case, an Australian redneck, the cry of the victim is always the same. It's often hard to explain the antagonist's motivation in the Horror genre but it's always easy to define the victim's: *survival*. Therefore, they often contain even less character growth than their genre cousin, the Thriller.

Written and directed by Greg Mclean — unofficial member of the "Splat Pack" which includes directors Alexandre Aja, Neil Marshall and Eli Roth — *Wolf Creek* is a simple but brutally effective horror.

A remote location is of primary importance to the horror genre, contributing in a big way to the victim's demise, and it's hard to think of anywhere more remote than the Australian outback. Some horrors like to grab the audience's attention with a shocking murder in the first scene. Others, such as *Wolf Creek* rely on the formula of first showing us relaxed good times in order to contrast as heavily as possible with the carnage to come.

Apart from a slight altercation with a bunch of rednecks in a bar, Wolf Creek's opening sequence contains absolutely zero conflict. For this reason, we have omitted from it all plot points. The Call to Action, therefore, is pushed back to Sequence B when the guys break down and meet Mick. The Big Event and introduction of true conflict then arises when Liz wakes up tied and bound and finds Kristy being tortured by Mick.

In this breakdown, Sequence D is effectively Sequence C when the girls escape, and Sequence E is really the Midpoint when Liz decides to return to the "Innermost Cave" of Mick's garage.

Here the stakes are raised when Liz finds Mick's souvenirs from previous murders and realizes the graveness of their situation in the obligatory "I'm going to hang around in the murderer's lair checking out stuff instead of getting the hell out" scene. Sequence E is effectively sacrificed in exchange for the "Good Times" first sequence, and we go straight to the All Is Lost moment with Kristy's murder.

By the end, there's only one survivor — Ben — and Mick is left free to kill again: a classic horror ending in which one character may have survived, but the evil lives on…

WOLF CREEK (2005)
SCREENPLAY BY GREG MCLEAN

ACT ONE
Sequence A – Kristy, Ben & Liz arrive at Wolf Creek

I

Super: Broome, Western Australia, 1999

At a car dealers, Ben buys a car. He drives off.

On the beach, two girls, Kristy and Liz, write postcards.

Ben tries to start the car with a mechanic.

The girls lie on the beach talking about Ben. They're leaving Australia.

Ben turns up and meets the girls. They want to get to Wolf Creek by tomorrow night.

II

The guys party at a house. Everyone jumps in the pool.

Liz wakes up the next morning on the beach next to the guys. She goes for a swim.

The guys drive off. Later, Liz drives and Ben plays the guitar.

That night, they camp out. Ben tells a story about a UFO.

The next morning, they pack up the tent and leave. Liz drives.

They arrive at Emu Creek. Kristy tells Ben Liz has a crush on him. She tells him to sort out whatever girlfriend he has in Sydney.

III

In the bar, a group of rednecks pick a fight with Ben. He leaves with the girls.

They drive through the outback and arrive at Wolf Creek: a walking trail. It'll take three hours and they set off.

Sequence B – The guys are rescued by Mick (- / +)

I

They look at a meteor crater. **(inciting incident)**
They rest. Liz goes for a walk. Kristy talks to Ben about the meteor.

Liz sits alone, looking at the crater. Ben joins her. They kiss and then laugh about it.

The guys pack up the car.

They have about an hour until dark. All of their watches have stopped. **(call to action)**

Plus the car won't start… **(negative big event)**

II

That night, they sit in the car, wondering about their watches and the car. They panic when they see lights, but it's a truck. Mick gets out.

Mick fixes their car. He's a little weird but friendly, and says the car's dead. **(midpoint)**

The guys debate whether to ask Mick if he wants money for helping them out. They don't have any. **(all is lost)**

III
Later, Mick says he'll tow them back to his place to fix it, for free. **(positive climax / screenplay call to action)**

Mick tows them into the darkness.

Sequence C – Liz realizes Mick wants to kill them (+ / -)

I
Later, they start to wonder where his place is as they've been driving for hours. **(inciting incident)**

They arrive at an old mining site. **(call to action)**

Later, they all sit around a campfire chatting. Mick talks about his old job killing animals. They all joke around. **(positive big event)**

II

Later, Liz falls asleep immediately. The other two are already asleep.

Next morning, Liz wakes up to find herself bound and gagged in a room. The others are nowhere in sight. **(midpoint)**

She uses a piece of glass to cut her ropes. She climbs out the window and finds the car engine in pieces.
She hears Kristy scream and sees her being tormented by Mick. **(all is lost / screenplay big event)**

III

Liz sets the car alight and lets off a gas canister. Mick arrives on the scene and realizes Liz has escaped. **(negative climax / screenplay big decision)**

ACT TWO
Sequence D – Liz & Kristy escape (- / +)

I

Liz gets to Kristy but Mick arrives again. **(inciting incident)**

Liz hides. Mick tortures Kristy again but Liz leaps out and shoots Mick. **(call to action)**

Liz can't reload the gun again to finish him off. She frees Kristy and they get in Mick's truck, but there are no keys... **(negative big event)**

II

Liz goes back to Mick's body and gets the keys. They start the engine but Mick shoots at them with a shotgun. They escape in the truck. **(midpoint)**

Mick follows them in a car. Liz stops the car at the edge of a cliff. **(all is lost)**

III

Liz and Kristy get out and push the truck over the edge. They crawl down the cliff. Mick arrives in his car and they hide. Mick heads down to look for the girls and they climb back up. **(positive climax / screenplay big event success)**

Sequence E – Mick kills Liz (+ / -)

I

Liz tells Kristy they have to go back to get a car. **(inciting incident)**

Ben's tied up at Mick's.

The girls arrive back. Liz makes Kristy wait and goes inside. **(call to action)**

She finds a fleet of cars. **(positive big event)**

II

Liz looks around at photos of all the people he's killed. She watches a videotape of Mick with other tourists. **(midpoint)**

Later, Liz starts a car… **(all is joy)**

III

But Mick is in the back seat and stabs her. He cuts off her fingers then severs her spine. **(negative climax / screenplay midpoint)**

Kristy calls out for Liz.

Sequence F – Mick kills Kristy (- / - -)

I

Kristy runs through the outback. She reaches the road and keeps running. **(inciting incident)**

She flags down a car. A man gets out and helps her. **(call to action)**

He's shot by a sniper rifle. Mick has Kristy in crosshairs. She sees Mick driving towards her and drives off. **(negative big event)**

II

Mick chases her but gets a flat tire and is forced to pull over. **(midpoint)**

She drives on, but he shoots out her tires and she crashes. **(all is lost)**

III

Mick waits for her to crawl out the wreckage and shoots her dead. **(negative climax / screenplay all is lost)**

Mick sets fire to the car.

ACT THREE
Sequence G – Ben survives (+ / + +)

I

Ben wakes up and realizes he's been nailed to a cross. **(inciting incident)**

He manages to free himself. **(call to action)**

Outside, he bandages up his wounds and escapes into the bush. **(positive big event)**

II

Later, Ben sleeps in the bush. **(midpoint)**

The next morning, Ben is rescued by two tourists. They drive him off.
(all is joy)

III

Ben is put on a medical airplane.

He is taken away by police.

Super: after four months, Ben is cleared of all suspicion. **(positive climax / screenplay climax)**

Mick walks off into the outback sunset. **(screenplay dénouement)**

FINAL WORDS & RESOURCES

Thank you once more for purchasing and reading this book. We hope it's been helpful in deepening your understanding of structure and made writing your current or next screenplay that little bit easier. We appreciate there's a lot of info to take on board here — especially if you're not familiar with sequences in the first place — so it may be well worth reading the book a couple of times to make sure you've really mastered the concepts.

Then, the fun begins… applying sequences to your own screenplay.

Overall, there are three main points to remember:

1. When plotting your movie, write a paragraph about what happens in each sequence and, most importantly, what happens at the Climax. Use each sequence to tell its own story, but in a way that moves the overall story forward.

2. As we stated earlier, these sequences aren't set in stone, so don't get too hung up on following their beats exactly

and end up writing to a template. Absorb all the information, then write your story using sequences as a guide and reference point, rather than a strict roadmap. When it's done, you can go back and really tighten it up by adding a Call to Action and Midpoint, etc. to each sequence.

3. Even used at their most basic level, sequences will add two more major beats/climaxes to your structure (at the end of Sequences C and E) and give your screenplay more twists and turns if you make every sequence start on a positive and end on a negative, or vice-versa.

This is the formula most popular movies follow and so by using sequences in your work you're well on your way to emulating, and then joining, the best.

Below are a list of resources to further help in the development of your understanding of sequences:

1. **Write Outlines**. Writing down what happens on screen as you watch a film is perhaps the best way to fully understand sequences and structure in general. Pick movies that are relatively easy to break down, such as

straightforward "goal orientated" films like *Stranger Than Fiction*. We go into more detail about this exercise and others on dialogue, scenes, characters, theme, etc. in our course *Script Hackr*: http://www.scriptreaderpro.com/online-screenwriting-course/

2. **Read Other Script Consultants' Books**. These screenwriting instructors talk about sequences and you may find their work useful, although Chris Soth's material is quite expensive and Paul Gulino's book tends to waver in its level of analysis.

The Coffee Break Screenwriter by Pilar Allesandra
The Sequence Approach by Paul Joseph Gulino
Sequences by Chris Soth

If you liked this book and found it helpful, please spread the word! We'd really appreciate it. And don't hesitate to contact us at hello@scriptreaderpro.com if you have any questions regarding the concepts discussed in this book, or want to make any suggestions/comments.

Thanks again for taking the time to read this book. We look forward to reading your sequence-structured screenplays.

All the best,

Founder of Script Reader Pro
www.scriptreaderpro.com
You write. We Read. They Love

SCRIPT READER PRO